BENEATI

THE GREAT I

JOSEPH ARCH ADDRESSES THE FARM LABOURERS' STRIKE MEETING AT WHITNASH IN 1872.

BENEATH THE GREAT ELMS

JEAN FIELD

AN ILLUSTRATED HISTORY OF WHITNASH IN WARWICKSHIRE

BREWIN BOOKS

First published
by Brewin Books, Studley, Warwickshire, B80 7LG
in May 1993

Reprinted October 1997

This book is dedicated to the memory of my father Hurban William Box who was particularly fond of the Whitnash elms.

British Library Cataloguing in Publication Data.
A Catalogue record for this book is available from the British Library

ISBN 1 85858 012 9

**Typeset by Avon Dataset, Bidford on Avon, Warwickshire, B50 4JH
and made and printed by Supaprint (Redditch) Limited. Redditch.**

ACKNOWLEDGEMENTS

Mr Gerald Cox of Whitnash has made an enormous contribution to this book by describing many aspects of village history and allowing me unlimited access to his vast collection of Whitnash memorabilia. Nearly one third of the photographs appearing here originated from his material and I would like to thank Gerald and his wife Freda, not least for relating many anecdotes which have enlivened the text.

Much of my research was conducted in Warwickshire County Record Office. I would like to thank the County Archivist and the rest of the staff, especially Jerry Weber, the Chief Conservator, who took many of the photographs reproduced in this book.

Having lived in Whitnash for many years and having represented the town on various councils, both Councillor B. Kirton (Mayor of Whitnash) and Councillor M. Morris (Deputy Mayor) have been particularly helpful. I am grateful to them for giving so freely of their time.

I would also like to thank Gary Archer (Regional Information Officer, Leamington Library), Paul Bolitho (Ex-Local History Librarian, Warwick Library), Father B. Boyle (St Joseph's R.C. Church), Canon A. Gardner (Rector of Whitnash), Rev. M. Sawyer (Whitnash Methodist Church), and numerous other people, including Miss J. Greenwood and the head teachers of the Whitnash Schools (Briar Hill First, St Joseph's R.C. Combined, St Margaret's C. of E. Middle and Whitnash Combined).

Finally the contribution of my brother Ian A.H. Box has been invaluable. Not only has he loaned photographs which he took himself, but in a variety of ways he has given me the benefit of his considerable knowledge about Whitnash.

THE SOURCES OF PHOTOGRAPHS CAN BE IDENTIFIED BY THE FOLLOWING ABBREVIATIONS. Birmingham Reference Library (BL), George Billington (GB), Ian Box (IB), The late H.W. Box's Collection (HB), Gerald Cox (GC), Jean Field (JF), Frances Gibbs (FG), Valerie Jacobs (VJ), Jean Pailing (JP), Warwickshire County Record Office (WCRO).

BIBLIOGRAPHY

A History & Description of the Parish of Whitnash – Rev. J. R. Young 1865
Parishes of the Diocese of Worcester Vol. 1 – Miller 1889
Historic Warwickshire – J. T. Burgess 1893
Evening Memories – Sir Herbert Maxwell 1924
Unknown Warwickshire – Mary Dormer Harris 1924
Victoria County History of Warwickshire Vol. 6 – 1951
The Place Names of Warwickshire – Gover, Mawer, Stenton 1970
Warwickshire – Vivian Bird 1973
Trees and Shrubs of Britain – Reader's Digest 1981
Leamington Methodist Circuit 1837-1987 – Edited Bolitho 1987
Chronicle of the Twentieth Century – Longmans 1988
The English Way of Death – Julian Litten 1991
Whitnash Parish Magazines – 1859 to 1881 and 1923 to 1992
Kelly's Directory of Warwickshire
Spennell's Directory of Warwickshire
Various editions of the Leamington Spa Courier and Coventry Evening Telegraph

FRONT COVER AND FRONTISPIECE

This engraving, dominated by the ancient elm tree on the village green, was on the front page of the *ILLUSTRATED LONDON NEWS* of April 13th 1872. Such treatment by the quality magazine made Whitnash famous nationwide.

At that time farm labourers mostly led dreadful lives. The article accompanying the picture said,

"Their toil is great. Their remuneration is scanty. The hardships to which they are exposed are numerous; and worst of all, their prospects, when old age has overtaken them, are without hope."

On 29th March 1872, a Warwickshire Agricultural Labourers' Union had been formed, thanks largely to the efforts of Joseph Arch, a Methodist Lay-Preacher who lived in Barford. Around 200 workers (out of a total of two to three thousand) had gone on strike in Warwickshire to try to force all farmers to improve the weekly wage from 12 shillings to 15 shillings, including such allowances as beer. On the whole the strike was successful as publicity forced the deplorable conditions to be improved.

Whitnash was probably chosen as the venue for a strike meeting as it was rural, yet close to Leamington and easily accessible for some famous speakers.

The engraving shows some wonderful characters set against the striking background of St Margaret's Church and the half-timbered Glebe House. I could gaze at this illustration for hours and still notice fresh details, so skilful was the artist in capturing a moment in history.

BACK COVER

This photograph, kindly loaned by the famous railway historian R. J. Blenkinsop, shows the 14.40 Birkenhead to London Paddington train on 18th May 1952 as it approached Black Bridge at Whitnash. The train had left Leamington Station at 18.31 and locomotive No. 6018 *King Henry VI* was hauling an extremely long train of 14 or 15 coaches. Railway enthusiasts might like to note that this was the first King Class locomotive in green livery that Mr Blenkinsop had photographed, as after nationalisation for a few years locomotives of this class had been painted blue.

INTRODUCTION

"When I last walked to Whitnash, the great elms were still splendid with leaves but roaring and rocking in the autumn storm, and the grey green of their branches seemed mist-like, as one gazed up through them to the deep-grey sky. Of the ancient elm before the church, only the stump of the trunk is left. Whitnash has great black and white barns with bulging sides, and the thatch coated with velvet moss and the lichen-covered tiles showed a thousand hues in the sunlight."

So wrote Mary Dormer Harris in her book "Unknown Warwickshire", published in 1924. She went on to describe the church standing "on an ancient earthwork" and the "way by the Golf Club to Harbury, still over desolate country."

Perhaps Mary Dormer Harris would not recognise Whitnash today, for this village has grown into a town, with its own Mayor and as with other Warwickshire villages during the twentieth century, the population has increased steadily. In the first three decades, the population growth was small, but from the late thirties onwards, the number of residents soared.

However, miraculously, unlike other villages, Whitnash managed to preserve its identity and was not swallowed up by Leamington. Even today the spirit of the village has survived and there are numerous reminders of what life was like in days gone by. A small nucleus of half-timbered houses has survived and although many guide books of Warwickshire are dismissive of the place, if you know where to look, there is a wealth of interesting stories and wonderful characters to be enjoyed.

I was not born in Whitnash, but my family moved there when I was six months old. I remember the village before the huge growth in population caused so many changes. From an early age, my brother and I became interested in the history for our late father always wanted to write a historical guide himself and his collection of books, photographs and cuttings has provided me with much material.

Many of the rarer photographs in this book have been loaned to me by Gerald Cox, who for many years has collected "archives" connected with the village where his family had lived for generations. Strangely, Gerald and I lived only a few hundred yards from each other when children, but it is only recently that I have become friendly with his family. Over the years, Gerald and his wife Freda gave a home to such items as old parish magazines, workbooks and postcards and these have proved invaluable in the production of this work.

It is a strange thing, but even now, almost all those who have ever lived there, think fondly of Whitnash, no matter where they may live afterwards. What then is this elusive spirit of Whitnash? I freely admit I have always loved the place and in this book I hope to show you why.

THIS STRETCH OF WILD COUNTRY ON THE WEST BANK OF THE WHITNASH BROOK WAS ONCE AN IMPORTANT PLACE MANY CENTURIES AGO.

It is generally accepted that Whitnash was a settlement of the Ancient Britons, with the village most likely being near The Fosse Way, which road marks the southern boundary of the parish. In all probability, there was a larger native settlement in Whitnash than in Leamington and it has been suggested that St Margaret's Church stands on an artificial mound of great pagan significance, through which a leyline (prehistoric straight track) passes directly.

The site shown in this recent photograph was occupied by a great mill and dam in Medieval times and it is believed that the ruins still lie underneath the mounds of earth near the brook. (JF)

TODAY USED MAINLY BY RAMBLERS AND DOG-WALKERS, THIS BRIDGE OVER THE BROOK AND ANCIENT FOOTPATH LEADING INTO WHITNASH FROM RADFORD WAS ONCE A MOST IMPORTANT THOROUGHFARE. (Regia via inter Radeford et Wytenas 1285)

To the south of this track, there was once a holy well where, according to legend, the inhabitants of Whitnash took the church bell to be reconsecrated prior to its being transported to the site of the present church. The bell fell into the water and was lost, thereafter giving rise to the superstition that the future could be told by the submerged bell. Although the site was drained well over a century ago, the water from a small stream running into the brook was reputed to have magical powers and was much sought after.

My grandfather, a lifelong resident of Leamington, always used to refer to "Whitnash on the Ocean", as did many other people in the area until a few years ago. The well known legend may have helped to popularise the nick-name but for many generations of children and adults, Whitnash Brook was a special place – wonderful for picnics and games such as floating leaf boats, in the days before radio and television, when people devised their own entertainment. (JF)

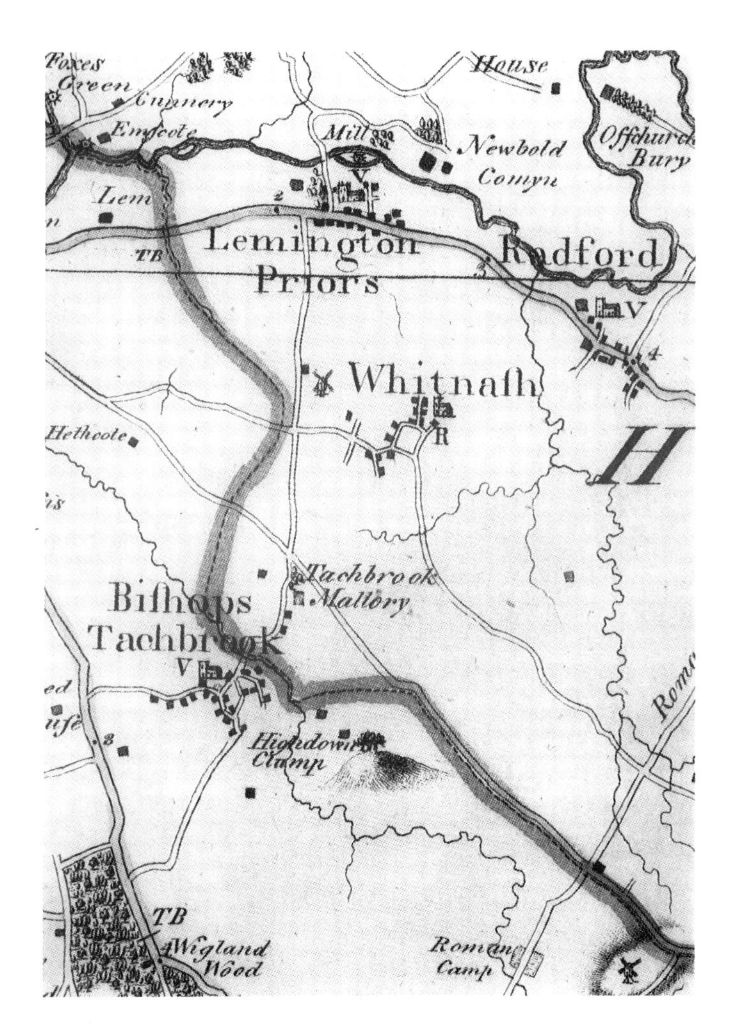

PART OF A MAP OF WARWICKSHIRE PRINTED IN 1793, THIS SHOWS THE AREA AROUND WHITNASH. For centuries, Whitnash and other nearby settlements had been larger and more important than Leamington, but in 1793 the population of the Spa was beginning to increase. The thick line through Bishop's Tachbrook marks the division between Kineton Hundred to the south and Knightlow Hundred (including Whitnash) to the north.

In his book "Warwickshire" Vivian Bird claimed that the Whitnash stretch of The Fosse Way was once the haunt of a highwayman named Bendigo Mitchell who operated north and south from Harwoods House. There were probably rich pickings to be had as travellers from Warwick joined The Fosse Way on the Whitnash boundary. (WCRO)

IN 1821 THE EARL OF AYLESFORD COMMISSIONED ACCURATE PICTURES OF ALL THE IMPORTANT BUILDINGS IN WARWICKSHIRE AND THIS PHOTOGRAPH IS OF THE PAINTING OF WHITNASH CHURCH FROM THE AYLESFORD COLLECTION, NOW HOUSED IN BIRMINGHAM REFERENCE LIBRARY.

In the reign of Henry 1 (1100 to 1135) St Margaret's Church was rebuilt and 18 acres of land were given to supply the Rector with an income. Unusually the church was not built exactly east to west, but appeared to be at angle consistent with the position of the rising sun on St Margaret's Day, July 20th. Until the nineteenth century, the Village Wake was always held on this day and much merrymaking accompanied the church's patronal festival.

The tower, now the oldest existing part of the building, was added in the late fifteenth century, probably by Benedict Medley of Warwick, Lord of the Manor of Whitnash from 1483 to 1503. Benedict Medley was Clerk of the Signet to King Henry Vll, but when he died, this important man was buried in the chancel of Whitnash Church, as was his wife. Their brasses can still be seen, now set into the south wall of the chancel.

The porch shown here was added in the eighteenth century, but was demolished before 1867, when the South Aisle and a new porch was built. (BL)

THIS IS WHAT THE INTERIOR OF ST MARGARET'S CHURCH WAS LIKE WHEN REV. YOUNG ARRIVED IN WHITNASH IN 1846. The walls of the ancient chancel were bulging out by around 14 inches at the top and had had to be reinforced. The cosy box pews (installed in 1795) were reserved for specific families by the paying of pew rents, the one nearest the chancel arch on the left belonging to the Cook family of the Manor House. The pew shown on the extreme left belonged to the Palmer family, that nearest the pulpit desk was reserved for the residents of Fosse Farm and the one on the extreme right belonged to the Wise family of Shrubland Hall. The seats in the chancel were used by the Rector's family and friends and a gallery at the rear of the church provided extra space.

In 1855 the chancel was rebuilt at the expense of the Rector, to designs by Sir George Gilbert Scott. Many original features were retained, such as the two stone memorials shown here on the chancel walls. The nave was not rebuilt until 1880, although the picturesque pulpit desk was replaced in 1861 and the entire church re-pewed in 1867.

This photograph is of a painting which is now housed in Warwickshire County Record Office. (WCRO)

THIS ROMANTIC VIEW OF THE GLEBE HOUSE WAS PORTRAYED IN A PAINTING DATED 1870. Many past Rectors lived in this house close to the church; the priest's door into the chancel being only a short distance across the churchyard.

The list of past Rectors* includes the names of some interesting people such as Nicholas Greenhill, one of the earliest Headmasters of Rugby School and Thomas Holyoake (1616–1675) who merits an entry in the "Dictionary of National Biography". During the Civil War he captained a foot company in Oxford for the King and after the Restoration, Lord Leigh made him Rector of Whitnash. Like his father, he was buried in St Mary's in Warwick.

In 1720 the Curate Humphrey Jones was buried in the churchyard in Whitnash, having been resident in the Glebe House. It is thereby presumed that he felt being Curate of Whitnash more important than being Vicar of Leamington, which position he also held. (WCRO)

* See Appendix

THIS OLD TREE WAS PROBABLY KNOWN TO WHITNASH RESIDENTS IN STUART, IF NOT ELIZABETHAN TIMES. Standing along the Tachbrook Road, near the boundary with Bishop's Tachbrook, this magnificent oak tree is one of the oldest living things in Whitnash. Measuring 21 feet around the trunk at a height of 5 feet, the tree must be at least 300 years old, probably much more. (JF)

JAMES REYNOLDS YOUNG M.A. WAS APPOINTED RECTOR OF WHITNASH IN 1846.

Born in London in 1807 and educated at Charterhouse School and Cauis College Cambridge, he was a fine classical scholar. A prominent churchman and an exceptionally good organiser, he was later created an Honorary Canon of Worcester Cathedral. He and his capable wife Mary Ann had 8 children in 10 years and the entire family helped him in his various ventures.

I could fill a complete book with the interesting life of this energetic man for amongst other things he organised the rebuilding of the crumbling church, ran a small Prep school in his new Rectory for the sons of the nobility and became an early amateur printer, installing a large printing press, which the boys in his school helped to run.

In 1869 after a serious illness, he went for a holiday to Ambleside in the Lake District, but whilst out walking on a steep path near Stock Ghyll Force, stepped on a wasp's nest and fell, breaking 2 ribs. Happily he recovered and was soon back at work again acting as Trustee for the village school, editing the Parish Magazines (complete with acrostic puzzles) helping to run a Clothing Club, Savings Bank and Working Men's Club, not to mention putting on Lantern Slide Shows, raising money for the rebuilding of the church and giving inspirational sermons.

Each of his enterprises helped others, for the wealthy parents of boys in his school donated items to the renovated church and on the printing press he produced "A History of Whitnash", religious tracts and lists of the Recitations his pupils performed each Christmas.

When he died in 1884 from congestion of the lungs, the whole village must have mourned and typically he left instructions that Walter Summerton, the village carpenter, was to make his coffin and organise his funeral. It was said that financially Canon Young gave more to the village than he received in stipend and the commemorative plaque in his church said "HE WAS A TENDER FATHER TO HIS PEOPLE". Certainly he loved Whitnash and did all he could to help its people.

If he was so clever, why did he choose to come to Whitnash? Many ask this and I believe the answer is that Whitnash was an ideal place for his school, being close to fashionable Leamington, besides being a most attractive and unspoilt place. Although he had great sympathy for his poorer parishioners, enthusiastic Canon Young was well-connected and his many talented friends, such as Miss Rachel Gray (the organist of Christchurch in Leamington), were pleased to help his cause in Whitnash.

I believe modern Whitnash owes a lot to Canon Young for he helped to foster a pride amongst the inhabitants that is still evident today. We have good cause to remember this charismatic, innovative and truly Christian man. (WCRO)

THIS IS A SECTION OF A BEAUTIFUL WOODCUT FEATURED ON THE COVERS OF WHITNASH PARISH MAGAZINES FROM 1859 TO THE EARLY 1880s. The old schoolhouse and original schoolroom can be seen in the centre (before the Infant Room was added in 1873) and Rose Cottage is on the left. The thatched row to the right was known as "The Barracks" (eventually demolished around 1939).

Whitnash was one of the first few parishes in the country to have a magazine, the first being issued in January 1859. Parish magazines were invented by Rev. J. Erskine Clarke of Lichfield who supplied 16 pages of general Christian interest, if clergymen could obtain a cover, printed locally, carrying local news. Canon Young, always keen on new ideas, had a large press installed at the Rectory and his pupils, family and a printer from "The Courier" on his day off, assisted him with the printing. The complete monthly magazine sold at 1½d a copy and the local pages only were ½d. In all probability, the enterprise lost money and with the death of Canon Young in 1884, the magazines ceased until 1919.

These old magazines now make fascinating reading – indeed the detail they carried was amazing. I believe that Canon Young as Editor hoped they would be useful to posterity and he even had copies placed in the cavity under the Foundation Stone of the new Nave of his church in 1880. Fortunately he also had back numbers of the local pages bound into special volumes costing 6s 6d each (9 years to a volume) entitled "Memorials of a Country Parish". I would dearly love to acquire such a volume, but they are extremely rare, as are single unbound covers. (WCRO)

IN 1865 MEDALS WERE STRUCK TO COMMEMORATE THE WHITNASH INDUSTRIAL EXHIBITION ORGANISED BY CANON YOUNG TO DEMONSTRATE THE EXCELLENT WORK CONNECTED WITH THE VILLAGE. Made by Joseph Moore of Birmingham, the medals bore the motto "Ora et Labora" meaning "Pray and Work". On sale at the exhibition itself, white metal medals cost 6d each, bronze ones with a leather case cost 2/6d whilst silver ones were 10 shillings each. An engraver attended the exhibition each day and visitors could have their medals engraved for 6d.

The Exhibition took place on St Margaret's Day, 20th July 1865 and also the following two days. A band played whilst the hundreds of visitors crowded the specially hired tent, the church and the Rectory garden. The catalogue which Canon Young had printed on the Rectory press makes fascinating reading. Serious historians can learn much from the hundreds of items listed, but my favourite exhibits were "The gloves of Charles 1 given by him on the scaffold to Bishop Juxton," and "Hair from Rev. J. R. Young, Mrs Young and family, arranged by Fraulein Haars." This young woman was a guest at the Rectory, but her offering seems a little odd by today's standards!

Having two 1865 originals in his possession, Gerald Cox had the brilliant idea of having 200 similar medals made to commemorate the Silver Jubilee of Queen Elizabeth 11 in 1977. Mr Cox naturally sent one to the Queen herself (receiving a letter of thanks from Buckingham Palace) and after an article in the local paper, the rest "sold like hot cakes", the profits going to local charities. (WCRO)

THE RECTORY CRICKET TEAM IN ACTION AROUND 1860. Most of the players were pupils of Canon Young's Prep School where the sons of the nobility enjoyed a sound, but liberal education.

Sir Herbert Maxwell in his book "Evening Memories" (published 1932) described how he attended Canon Young's School from 1855 to 1858. Stressing the kind, but firm nature of Canon Young, Herbert Maxwell loved the school, which catered for only 12 boys at a time.

Having described how Canon Young provided many worthwhile interests and how Mrs Young was kind, but quick tempered, he wrote,

"Both of these worthies crossed the bourne long ago; the rectory is no longer a school, but many a time do I stroll in fancy along the terrace overlooking the cricket ground, thread the moth-haunted shrubbery screening the kitchen garden and saunter along the green lane where the redstart used to nest." (WCRO)

"WHITNASH BROOK WAS FULL OF DELECTABLE CREATURES – MILLER'S THUMBS, MINNOWS AND HERE AND THERE AN ELUSIVE TROUTLET".

So wrote Herbert Maxwell in 1932 when he described the Whitnash he had known in 1855.

This photograph taken in 1958, brings back many happy memories to me of reading books when perched in old willow trees and paddling near Pebble Island.

Watercress, freshly gathered from the brook, was sold around the village on Sunday afternoons in the 1930s by "Cookie" – Mr Cook, a real old countryman who had the reputation of being a most humane chicken killer, when the deed needing doing. During the Second World War, when many of our families kept chickens, I watched him painlessly wring a chicken's neck in a few seconds.

A few decades ago, Gerald Cox too used to gather watercress, but his wife Freda recalled that unless it was washed thoroughly, the numerous small snails clinging to it made it taste gritty! (IB)

THIS DRAMATIC STRETCH OF ROAD, KNOWN TO SOME AS "THE FAIRY DELL" ONCE LINKED UPPER GOLF LANE WITH THE HARBURY LANE. Clearly marked on maps at the end of the nineteenth century, the road crossed the land bought by the Golf Club in 1908. It remained open as a footpath until the 1950s, when the right of way beyond the isolated section shown in this recent photograph was finally lost. (JF)

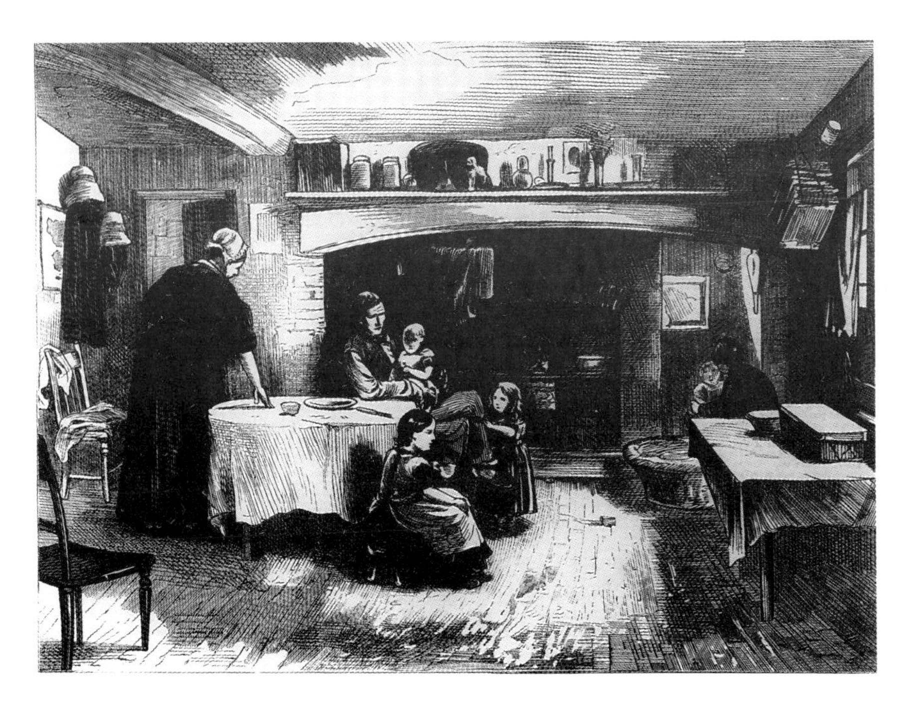

SPARSELY FURNISHED, BUT CLEAN AND TIDY, THIS LABOURER'S COTTAGE IN WHITNASH WAS DEPICTED IN *THE ILLUSTRATED LONDON NEWS* OF APRIL 13th 1872. In the nineteenth century, many of the poor lived drab lives, unable to afford even the basics of life, even though they worked long hours.

For many winters, kindly Canon Young arranged for rice and haricot beans to be purchased in bulk from Liverpool Docks so that the poorer families could buy subsistence rations when the potato and fruit crops had failed.

"Notice will be given of the sale of the rice, as soon after it arrives as may be, by ringing the church bell. The cottagers are requested to bring bags, cloths or basons for carrying it away," announced the Parish Magazine of December 1879. In 1881, the magazine carried details of how the rice and beans were sold to needy families at half the cost price, rice being 1d and beans 1½d per pound. Canon Young even included a recipe for cooking the beans.

"The villagers will remember how excellent the haricots were in former years, when properly cooked, that is, steeped in water for 12 hours, then stewed with a piece of bacon or other savoury meat."

It was small wonder that many poor people died young and it was a sobering thought that in 1861, when a special dinner was given at the Rectory and a fatted sheep was killed, the aged inhabitants of the village were invited – those over 50 years of age. (WCRO)

ELIZABETH SOPHIA (SOPHY) LANDOR, PHOTOGRAPHED AROUND 1860, WAS LADY OF THE MANOR FROM 1866 TO 1889. Born in 1815, the niece of Walter Savage Landor the poet, Sophy often cared for her uncle Henry Eyres Landor who lived in The Manor House at Bishops's Tachbrook. Henry had bought the Manor House in Whitnash in 1826 and he also owned Whitnash property which had belonged to his Eyres family ancestors. Being a wealthy land agent, he was generous to the people of Whitnash and Tachbrook, amongst other things giving 30 pairs of blankets to the poor of each village each winter. In 1860 he gave land and money for the school at Whitnash and when he died Sophy inherited his Whitnash lands and responsibilities. (WCRO)

RUTH ISOBEL YOUNG, BORN IN 1850, WAS THE SECOND DAUGHTER OF CANON YOUNG. Like her four brothers and three sisters, Ruth helped considerably with parish affairs. She was a skilled artist and raised much money for the restoration of St Margaret's Church by completing watercolours and selling them. On their birthdays, she and her sisters used to entertain the children of the village at the Rectory and on 31st July 1871 Ruth hosted a party for over 130 children. Following tea on the terrace, games in the Rectory field and the presentation of a gift (made by Ruth) to each child, proceedings ended at nightfall with "Hearty cheers for Ruth Young". (WCRO)

TAKEN IN THE 1860s, THIS EARLY PHOTOGRAPH WELL ILLUSTRATES THE STATE OF THE VILLAGE GREEN IN WINTER TIME. The proximity of the Glebe House to the church can be appreciated, as can the age of the elm to the right. The village stocks once stood near the elm and Canon Young told how they were in common use until around 1825.

I always like to think of the Glebe House on November 2nd 1880, which was Canon Young's 73rd birthday and the day the new Nave was dedicated. For the Afternoon Service (fully choral) 12 Clergy and 18 choir members robed in the Glebe House and processed into the church via the main door, singing "Onward Christian Soldiers." That procession across the churchyard, with 30 men and boys in surplices, must have given Canon Young a great sense of achievement with the church building then fully restored.

Less than 4 years after that date, Canon Young died aged 76, and it would appear that the half-timbered Glebe House was demolished not long afterwards. (WCRO)

THIS PHOTOGRAPH SHOWS A PAINTING OF THE OLD RECTORY, BUILT IN 1847. The front door faced north and Margaret Gleave (now Mrs Lomas) the daughter of Rev. Gleave (Rector from 1935-67) said that she was always told that the key-hole in that door was level with the top of the flag-pole on the Parish Church in Leamington.

Mrs Lomas wrote, "The Rectory had a vast garden and as well as goats and bees, we also kept chickens, ducks and geese. The geese were a great help in keeping the grass down when petrol was rationed and the lawn mower could not be used. One of the lawns could comfortably hold two tennis-courts and with a motor mower it involved walking over five miles every time it was mown. This lawn was an ideal setting for Church Fetes. On Rogation Sunday, (weather permitting) the Choir and congregation processed from Church to hold the second half of the Evening Service on the top terrace of the Rectory garden, overlooking a large amount of the parish, in those days mainly green fields. The new Rectory was built (in 1958) on the partly walled vegetable garden of the old Rectory and the site of the old house now holds five bungalows." (WCRO)

THIS MUCH ADMIRED PHOTOGRAPH, WHICH WAS TAKEN AROUND 1860 FROM NEAR "THE PLOUGH AND HARROW", SHOWS THE ENTRANCE TO GOLF LANE ON THE RIGHT AND GLAMIS COTTAGE TO THE LEFT. The other houses to the left were demolished many years ago, but they do feature on some early photographs. It is possible, although unlikely, that the timber to the right is a pile of telegraph poles. The villagers, farm cart and the horse and carriage all help to make this a memorable scene. (GC)

TAKEN FROM THE OPPOSITE ANGLE, A LITTLE FURTHER DOWN THE SAME STRETCH OF ROAD AS THAT DEPICTED ON THE PREVIOUS PAGE, GLAMIS COTTAGE IS SHOWN BEHIND THE HORSE AND TRAP. The Homestead Farmhouse (now "Elderfield") is on the left and the half-timbered barn (demolished in the 1950s) belonged to Home Farm. Interestingly, when the barn was being demolished, a boy walking home from Whitnash School spotted an old clay pipe in a hollow in the brickwork. Perhaps hidden by a farm worker in Victorian times, this pipe is an amusing relic of old Whitnash.

Today maisonettes occupy the site of the barn and the entrance to Palmer Road is on the right.

(GC)

THE OLD SCHOOL BUILDINGS HAVE NOT CHANGED THAT MUCH SINCE THIS PHOTOGRAPH WAS TAKEN IN 1904. The school house, complete with bell, is shown on the left, with the Junior Room in the middle and the Infant Room (added in 1873) to the right. The headmistress, Mrs Morris, is on the left and her assistant, Miss Taylor, to the right.

In 1860, Henry Eyres Landor, the wealthy Lord of the Manor, donated this school for the children of the village, giving land and an endowment of £1,200. The original building, costing around £800, had only one classroom and no water laid on, so the pupils had to use primitive earth closets. Not until 1938 was the school house connected to mains water and sewers.

In the later 1940s there were about 90 pupils accommodated in 3 classes in the old building. Mrs (Bateman) Jones was the headmistress and teacher of the Upper Juniors, Mrs Lambert was the teacher of the Lower Juniors and the long-serving Mrs Nichols the Infants teacher. I can see her now thumping away on the piano as the percussion (we called it "pincushion") band clanged noisily around her.

Eventually the school could not cope with rising numbers and in 1956 a new County Junior School opened in Langley Road. A new C. of E. Infant and Junior School was built in Coppice Road in 1964 and this is now St Margaret's Middle School. There are 230 pupils and Mr Alan Jones is the head teacher.

The original school buildings have been used as a Church Centre since 1964 and Mr and Mrs Dyson, who live in the old school house, are the present custodians. (GC)

THIS SCHOOL GROUP TAKEN OUTSIDE WHITNASH SCHOOL AROUND 1905, SHOWS THE HEADMISTRESS, MRS MORRIS TO THE LEFT AND MISS TAYLOR TO THE RIGHT.

In April 1910, Mrs Morris retired as Headmistress, after having been in the post for 21 years and her leaving presents included a gold watch from "friends in the parish".

The Headmistress during the 1920s and 1930s was Miss Tooth who retired in 1939 when Miss Davies (later Mrs Bateman-Jones and Mrs Rogers) from Aberfan in Wales, was offered the post. (GC)

A PLOUGHING MATCH AROUND 1900, WHICH APPEARS TO HAVE TAKEN PLACE IN WHITNASH, IN A FIELD OFF GOLF LANE.

In former times, the fields in Whitnash had romantic names such as Black Feathers Meadow, Fox Beard, Longfurlong, Ninelands, Rowley Field, Whitmore, Brier Hill Field, Grange Hill, Horse Pool Meadow, Mill Dam Meadow and Twenty Acres Field.

Whitnash was one of the last places in England to have the fields enclosed and when the common land was lost to the poorer inhabitants, Allotment Gardens were provided at small rents. Four acres of land were set aside "for the Labouring Poor of the Parish" and tenants had to pay 6d per perch, per annum, quarterly in advance. The size of the plots varied from 12 to 17 perches and when one fell vacant, numerous applications were received. In Victorian times, there were many rules attached to the tenure – amongst them that "No tenant should work on his garden on a Sunday." (WCRO)

LOOKING TOWARDS GREEN FARM AROUND 1907, THIS PHOTOGRAPH (LABELLED 'LANDOR'S COTTAGES') SEEMS TO CAPTURE THE SPIRIT OF VILLAGE LIFE. Close examination reveals Mr Watts the baker delivering bread, an ancient baby carriage outside the cottage door and a host of curious children, obviously coming out of school.

I always knew Landor's Cottages as "Larner's Cottage" and I am now convinced that we pronounce the name Landor wrongly. Scholars have suspected that the name should be pronounced "Larnder" and I believe the probable corruption "Larner" reinforces this view.

For many years the cottages were inhabited by the Watts family, hence in more recent times they were known as "Watts Cottages." (WCRO)

WAS THE WOMAN OUTSIDE GREEN FARM GARDENING OR CHATTING TO SOMEONE INSIDE? Apparently taken around 1900, this photograph shows the gate to the Manor House to the right and the attractive cottages in the main road on the left. These two cottages, which until a few years ago, had a traditional cottage-style garden in front, are now joined into one substantial, half-timbered property. (GC)

150 YEARS AGO IT WAS SAID THERE WERE MORE TREES THAN HOUSES IN THE MAIN STREET AND EVEN THIS SCENE, PHOTOGRAPHED ABOUT 1900, IS DOMINATED BY THE TREES AND HEDGES. These houses in Woodbine Terrace near Avon Road were the most outlying in the village (apart from 10 in Heathcote Terrace and a couple of isolated larger dwellings) and Heathcote Road was still a country lane.

In the 1930s, Tabor's Dairy (later Felgate's in the 1950s) was situated to the right of the houses and during the Second World War, the fire station was to the right of the shop. Today three of the houses in Woodbine Terrace still remain and the flats of Glebe Court occupy the site to the right. (GC)

THESE TWO PHOTOGRAPHS TAKEN AROUND 1900 ARE INTERESTING BECAUSE OF THE PEOPLE. The top view shows Chapel Yard with many of the houses with half drawn blinds, probably to exclude the sun as was the custom. Mrs Tozer (left) and Miss Tozer are shown in the foreground. These houses still remain today, Chapel Yard (now known as South Terrace), being a secluded cul-de-sac, behind Field Views. (GC)

The lower view is of the corner of Avon Road and the children seem a really happy bunch. The two girls in the road have skipping ropes and the bicycle seems surprisingly modern. The large house on the corner still remains, although somewhat altered in appearance. (GC)

THE WHITNASH FOOTBALL TEAM OF 1910–11 OBVIOUSLY TOOK THEIR FOOTBALL SERIOUSLY. One of the cups shown here is the Whitnash Charity Cup, won on 30th April 1910, when Whitnash beat Spencer Street in the final. All proceeds from this cup went to help the poor of the village. I could find no record of the other cup – it may have been the Garland Invitation Cup.

Mr Fred Meades, now living in Coventry but born and brought up in Whitnash around 80 years ago, laughed as he told me how his father had been in the Charity Cup winning team of 1910. He said as a boy he was always told that the team had to get the goal-posts out of pawn before each match! Certainly from local newspaper reports of the time, I found the team shown in this photograph was decidedly impoverished and a concert was held in the village to help raise funds.

(GC)

WHEN THE LEAMINGTON AND COUNTY GOLF CLUB OPENED THE GOLF COURSE IN WHITNASH IN 1908, IT CAUSED MANY CHANGES IN THE VILLAGE. As early as March, the Parish Council was worried about the great increase in motor traffic in Golf Lane, but many villagers welcomed the course as it offered opportunities for employment. By June 1908, the first six holes out and the last four home had been completed and 15 of the greens had been seeded, dressed with malt dust and sand and drained. A gang of men, such as these shown here, had mowed the greens to a width of 60 yards.

This photograph may have been taken at that time or perhaps slightly later. It is believed that the man holding the head of the horse on the left is Ted Young, with Bert Bayliss holding the flag, George Cotterill with the hand mower in the centre and Toddy Parker holding the centre horse. (GC)

THIS PHOTOGRAPH OF THE CLUB HOUSE WAS TAKEN SOON AFTER ITS CONSTRUCTION IN 1908. According to the 'Leamington Spa Courier' of that year, altogether the Club House cost £1,434, counting £1,200 for the building itself and an additional £234 for the well and other necessities. The furnishing of the house cost £300 and in June 1908 it was estimated that the course would cost £1,200 to complete, plus another £550 for rates, machinery and compensation for tenants, At that time only £1,900 had been promised, but many of the members agreed to pay their subscriptions early (Entrance Fee of £3 for the 300 males and £2 for the 220 females, with an Annual subscription of £3 Guineas for both sexes) to help finances.

The course was designed and constructed under the supervision of Mr H. S. Colt of Sunningdale and in 1934, he supervised modernisation. During World War Two, 8 holes were turned over to food production and after the war, Hawtree and Son carried out further extensive modernisation, the course being re-opened in 1952.

In 1990 the Club House was rebuilt, but the original, distinctive, gabled section was retained. Today there are around 650 members and the course is amongst the finest in the Midlands. (WCRO)

THE BUGLER SOUNDS THE LAST POST, WHILST THE RECTOR, REV. C. A. H. RUSSELL (IN SURPLICE TO THE RIGHT) STANDS WITH LORD LEIGH AND MANY OF THE POPULATION OF THE VILLAGE. This service apparently took place when the War Memorial was dedicated, probably in the summer of 1920, for the old elm is in full leaf and many of the crowd are wearing straw hats. This dramatic photograph is amongst my favourites for it seems to capture a very moving moment in the life of the village. (GC)

THIS VIEW OF THE VILLAGE GREEN IN 1922 REMINDS ME OF HARD PEARS AND DELICIOUS, FRESHLY-BAKED BREAD. In the 1940s Sam Watt's bakery on the extreme left was a delightful place where children on their way home from the village school could buy a crusty roll, or in summer 4 fallen pears, for one old penny. Gerald Cox recalled how he helped Mr Watts on Saturdays during the 1940s, when trays of loaves were often put to cool on the green. Of the buildings in this photograph only the ivy-clad Cooks Cottages and Green Farm House remain today. (GC)

THE ANCIENT ELM IN FRONT OF THE CHURCH DOMINATED THIS SCENE IN THE 1920s. Most elm trees in England were planted in the seventeenth or eighteenth centuries, but this tree was far older than that, perhaps being planted when the church tower or even the ancient church was built. In December 1872, a fierce gale had damaged the upper branches and in 1908, protective railings had been erected to prevent children clambering inside "ole holler". Fertility rites may have been connected with it for in 1960, Mrs Emma Golby, aged 81, said, "The old folk of the village used to say that when the tree came down, there would be no more babies here." (WCRO)

THIS PHOTOGRAPH SHOWS THE WHITNASH BIBLE CLASS OF 1923. Those present from left to right were – STANDING – Rose Newton, William Smith, Unknown, Mrs Russell (wife of Rector) Alfred Thomas Cox and D. Owen. SITTING – Joyce Bailey, Kathleen Hall, Mary Bennett, Rev. C. A. H. Russell (Rector) Miriam Treadwell, Lois Reading and Emily Bayliss. I wonder if the beautiful black cat which is sitting on Miriam's lap lived at the Rectory? (GC)

THIS PHOTOGRAPH, TAKEN IN 1922, IS FROM THE COLLECTION OF GERALD COX AND IT SHOWS HIS BROTHER BILL AS THE MAY KING AND PHIL DEVANNEY AS THE QUEEN. From the left the names of the other children are – Alice Boneham, Dot Golby, Ethel Mockford, Alf Newton, with Dorothy Owen, Unknown and Annie Ovard to the right of the cart. The children are standing near the entrance to the old Rectory Drive and one of the original gateposts (still in existence today) can be seen to the left. (GC)

THIS PRETTY YOUNG WOMAN, KATE COX, ACTED AS THE VILLAGE NURSE FOR MANY YEARS. Pictured here aged 21, soon after she had moved to Whitnash from Harbury, Kate soon became a very well respected figure in the village. Married in Whitnash Church in 1912, Kate learned her nursing skills in the time-honoured way – from assisting others.

It is hard to imagine Whitnash with few telephones and no Doctors' Surgery, but during the first half of the twentieth century it was often difficult to summon medical aid in a hurry. From delivering babies to laying out the dead, the village nurse carried out a wide variety of duties vital to the well-being of the inhabitants.

During the Second World War, Kate, then living in Lammas Terrace, close to the First Aid Station, helped to provide essential medical cover, working closely with Mrs Cuthbert and Mrs Russell of the Red Cross. After enjoying some years of retirement, Kate died in 1977 aged 85 and was buried in Whitnash Cemetery.

As he described these details to me recently, it was evident that Gerald Cox had been very proud of his mother. (GC)

THERE ARE SOME INTERESTING STORIES CONNECTED WITH THIS WHITNASH CHURCH CHOIR GROUP IN 1924. There are 3 generations of the Bayliss family and 2 generations of the Hauley and Chimes family represented here.

From left to right the back row is Bill Markham, unknown, unknown, Ted Billington, Fred Meades, Len Newton, unknown, Bert Bayliss. Second row – Major Chimes (with cross), unknown, Mr Fred Hauley (choir member from 1919 to 1963), Miss Parker (organist), Mr Chimes, unknown, Mr Bayliss (Junior), Mr Whitehead (with cross).

Seated – Mr Hauley (Junior), unknown, unknown, Rev. E. Bryan (Rector), Mr Bayliss (Senior), Walter Maynard, Charles Webb. Front row – George Billington, unknown, C. Spanswick, Denis Mockford, with the other boys being unknown.

Three years after his appointment Rev. Bryan had to endure the death of his wife Irene in December 1926. She was only 54 and her grave is situated next to that of Rev. A. M. Russell (a previous Rector) to the left of the path near the gate in the cemetery down Church Lane. In 1929 Major Chimes died at the age of 69 and he was buried close by. (GB)

ONE COLD WINTER'S EVENING, WHEN I WAS ELEVEN YEARS OLD, I FIRST WALKED UP THE DRIVE TO THIS MANOR HOUSE. OWLS HOOTED IN THE OVERHANGING TREES NEAR THE GATE AND I REMEMBER BEING STARTLED TO SEE TWO HUGE EYES PEERING DOWN AT ME.

The Manor House, with the half-timbered gabled section dating from the seventeenth century, was situated to the right of Green Farm. Seen here in a photograph taken in the 1920s, it had been partially rebuilt in the early nineteenth century.

Mrs Frances Gibbs of Avon Road worked at the Manor House for nearly twenty years and she recalled that in the 1930s, when she arrived from Birmingham, the tenant George Masters and his wife, took in paying guests during the summer months. "I used to have to get up at 5 o'clock in the morning," laughed Mrs Gibbs, but I could tell by the way she spoke that she had enjoyed her time there. "During the Second World War, Mrs Masters used to collect German and Italian Prisoners of War to help work the farm" she recalled, but when the house was demolished in 1959, after the death of Mr and Mrs Masters, she acknowledged she cried.

Today the site is occupied by Greenhill Road and Mr and Mrs Norman (long-standing Whitnash residents who now live in one of the houses) told me that when they first moved in, the electricity meter from the Manor Farm Dairy was still in their lounge! (WCRO)

MAY DAY CELEBRATIONS WERE AN IMPORTANT PART OF VILLAGE LIFE AND THIS PHOTOGRAPH, PROBABLY TAKEN IN THE 1920s IS A TOUCHING REMINDER OF THIS.

The patient donkey steals the scene, whilst the small king and queen sit in the magnificently decorated trap. (WCRO)

SOUTH FARM POND, OTHERWISE KNOWN AS "THE PIT" HAS LONG SINCE DISAPPEARED, BUT THE HOUSES OF "FIELD VIEWS" ON THE LEFT STILL REMAIN. Only the half-timbered cottage on the right is still standing – that which was the Vestry Clerk's Cottage, until the 1920s. This snapshot of the area round "The Plough and Harrow" was probably taken in the 1920s, before the houses in Heathcote Road were built.

In the past the pond itself was a vital part of village life. Mr Fred Meades related to me recently how youths would skate on it in hard winters when it was frozen and it was said that a certain man who lived nearby would swim in it each August Monday – parting the green slime as he did so.

During the 1940s, Mrs Franklin, the wife of the South Farm farmer, gave lessons in elocution. Jean Addicott (now Mrs Pailing) said that sometimes, when a child, she was too scared to attend for her lesson as the geese near the pond attacked her as she walked past. As for me, I have very unpleasant memories of the pond in 1947, when some louts snatched a loaf I had been sent to buy from Mr Watts' bakery and threw it into the pond for a laugh.

When the pond was drained and houses built on the site, the water had to be culverted across Golf Lane and down to the brook. It seems likely that the ancient pond had been fed from an underground spring. (JP)

THIS VIEW OF THE "PLOUGH AND HARROW" CORNER IN THE 1930s, BEFORE THE HOUSES IN HEATHCOTE AND WHITNASH ROAD WERE BUILT, SEEMS DOMINATED BY THE DELIGHTFUL BLACK AND WHITE COTTAGE ON CHAPEL GREEN. For many years "The Cottage" was inhabited by John Cotterill and his family; he living to be 95 and still digging his garden at the age of 92. The "Leamington Morning News" of January 14th 1957 carried an inspiring article about John and his wife Sarah. "Plenty of exercise ... that's what you need. I worked on the railways for nearly forty years and I always walked to the job," he was quoted as saying. Said to have been born in "The Cottage", in later years "Jack" had been the groundsman at Warwick School.

When he died in February 1960, John Cotterill was buried in Whitnash Cemetery, but sadly his unusual cottage did not survive for long. Needing many repairs, it was offered to the Parish Council, who felt unable to accept it because of the cost of renovation. Eventually, it was pulled down – an act that saddened my father to his dying days, as he and others had fought long and hard to save the seventeenth century property, with its distinctive wooden-rail decoration. (WCRO)

THIS INTERESTING OLD HOUSE ONCE STOOD ISOLATED IN A FIELD AND WAS APPROACHED BY THE LANE OPPOSITE TO HOME FARM.

Fred Meades related a curious tale concerning this house in the 1920s. Following a fire in the thatch, the Treadwell family, who had lived in the house for many years, fixed an old galvanised bucket over the chimney in an effort to stop sparks causing further mishaps. "It looked very funny," he chuckled, but no doubt it was logical and effective.

In the 1940s and 1950s, the house was inhabited by eccentric Mrs Osborne and this photograph was taken shortly before partial rebuilding in 1959. Today, the distinctive gable on the right still remains and the house is surrounded by far newer properties in Home Farm Crescent. (IB)

UNTIL THE 1950s, HOME FARM WAS A WORKING FARM AND THIS VIEW SHOWS HALF-TIMBERED STABLES AND A BARN TO THE LEFT, WITH PIG AND CALF PENS TO THE RIGHT. This photograph was taken (around 1900?) from the field known as "The Knob" on the other side of the road, hence the expanse of hedge in the foreground. It would appear that harvesters, complete with mowers and threshing machines, are posing in front of the house. (GC)

THIS CLOSE UP OF THE HOUSE (TAKEN AROUND 1920?) REVEALS MANY INTERESTING DETAILS SUCH AS THE MILK CHURNS IN THE YARD AND THE RAIL FOR TETHERING HORSES IN FRONT OF THE WALL.

Home Farm dates mainly from the seventeenth century and the date 1652 is carved into a beam. The dining room has fine timber panelling and for much of this century, farmer Ernest Masters and other family members were in residence.

I was much amused a few years ago when a newspaper report called this fine half-timbered farmhouse a "mock-tudor mansion". Someone's historical knowledge was sadly lacking!

(GC)

THE EERIE HALF LIGHT AND SNOW-COVERED HOLLOW ELM TREE IN THIS DICKENSIAN TYPE SCENE SENDS SHIVERS DOWN MY SPINE. I muse on Christmases long past and think of carol singers.

In recent times, Whitnash residents such as Bill and Linda Pound playing melodeons, have accompanied the carol singers as they performed around the town. Thus the traditional Christmas activities, no doubt carried out by hundreds of village folk over the centuries, have been kept alive. (IB)

IN ST MARGARET'S CHURCH THERE ARE MANY FINE EXAMPLES OF STONE CARVING BY MISS AGNES BONHAM, A YOUNG FRIEND OF CANON YOUNG. Although the angel on the front has been damaged, this pulpit (erected in 1862) is still extremely beautiful. (JF)

THIS MIDLAND RED BUS OF THE 1930s IS OUTSIDE GREEN FARM BARN OPPOSITE TO DOGLANDS LANE. In the early days buses stopped near the church, but later the route was extended to the "Plough and Harrow". Gerald Cox recalls that when he lived nearby as a boy, he would often help the bus-driver re-start the engine which had to be cranked with a huge handle. After more houses had been built, the route was extended to Heathcote Terrace. (GC)

REV. C. H. GLEAVE, RECTOR FROM 1935 TO 1967, STRIKES AN INFORMAL POSE IN THIS SNAPSHOT DATING FROM THE LATE 1930s. The name of the woman on the left is unknown, but next to Rev. Gleave is businessman and keen organist Mr G. Gibbs. Mrs Gibbs is next to her husband and Mrs Gleave is on the right. (GC)

THIS WOODEN HUT, WHICH ONCE STOOD ON THE CORNER OF FRANKLIN ROAD AND HEATHCOTE ROAD, HAD QUITE A HISTORY. It began as builder Mr Montgomery's Site Office and recently Olive and George Billington described to me how in that very same hut, on a snowy day in January 1939, they paid a £2 deposit for their home in Franklin Road. Younger readers might be amazed to learn that the full price of the semi-detached house was £595 – the mortgage repayments working out at only 13/6 (67½p) per week! During the Second World War the hut was used as the First Aid Post and this snap obviously dates from that era.

For a number of years Franklin Road ended at Number 10, a popular caravan site occupying the ground at the end of the road. A nightingale could often be heard singing in Mrs Clements' orchard nearby and many visitors came hoping to hear it. (GC)

THIS SNAPSHOT SHOWS A SECOND WORLD WAR AMBULANCE OUTSIDE THE FIRST AID POST IN FRANKLIN ROAD. The boys showing an interest are Nigel Cuthbert (right), Gordon Dingley (front), Terry Percox (behind), with an unknown boy on the left. (GC)

WELL DO I REMEMBER ATTENDING A PERFORMANCE OF "THE GHOST TRAIN" IN THIS SEEMINGLY ORDINARY CHURCH HALL. THE RATHER RICKETY STAGE WOBBLED AT TIMES AND THE SCENERY SHOOK, BUT WE STILL APPLAUDED "THE WHITNASH PLAYERS" OF 1949 TO THE ECHO.

Opened on November 16th 1922, by Alderman Davis of Leamington, St Margaret's Hall was situated on a site in Whitnash Road, opposite to the Doglands Lane. Major Chimes (one of the Churchwardens) having supervised its erection, on the opening day there were over 800 visitors, as the opening ceremony was followed by a concert and dance.

For a number of years, it was the only hall in the village and so was the venue for a variety of events from the Sunday School to Public Meetings. The village school used it as a dining room (happy memories of the day in 1948 when the wrong canisters were delivered from the school canteen and we ended up with no dinner, but five times our quota of jam tarts and custard!) and later as an additional schoolroom when the number of pupils increased rapidly.

For many years, until the late 1960s, this hall played a major part in the lives of residents of all ages. (GC)

FOR VARIOUS REASONS, I FIND THIS SNAP OF BILL MASTERS' RICK YARD PARTICULARLY EVOCATIVE. The corner of St Margaret's Hall is shown on the left and this reminds me of the connection between Whitnash and "The Archers" radio serial.

On October 10th 1942 a Harvest Supper was held in the church hall and speeches made then, fired enthusiasm for closer links between the country and town. The Minister of Agriculture later that year wrote, "That Harvest Home will, I trust, be but the beginning of a great movement to bring town and countryside in close and abiding relationships, leading to a greater mutual recognition and appreciation of each other's problems." This same spirit in 1951 gave rise to "The Archers" serial, which was designed to familiarise people with the problems of a rural community.

This scene also reminds me of a terrible trick which Bill Masters once played on me. On the pretext of giving me a drink of warm milk, he and his son persuaded me to visit his milking shed, where they sprayed me with milk straight from the cow's udder! I suspect this trick was often played on children and "townies."

This snap was taken around 1955, but today the Whitnash Road site opposite the Doglands looks entirely different. (IB)

FOR CENTURIES "THE PLOUGH AND HARROW" WAS THE ONLY INN IN WHITNASH. The oldest part of the building dates from the seventeenth century and this can be seen in the centre of this recent photograph.

In the past the Innkeeper was also a farmer in possession of several fields and Fred Meades, George Billington and others remembered that until around 1930, a fair was sometimes held behind the inn.

Younger readers may not appreciate the relief and happiness expressed at the end of the Second World War and Richard Hassan and others told me of the wonderful celebrations which took place near "The Plough" on V.E. night – 8th May 1945. Walter Hassan rigged up some lights, a piano was transported there on Ernie Masters' cart and George Billington took along his drum kit. Jack Cotterill at one time feared for the thatch of his nearby cottage as a huge bonfire showered sparks into the night sky. At that party, as at numerous others in Whitnash, the singing and dancing went on well after midnight. (JF)

IF EVER A PHOTOGRAPH CAPTURED THE ATMOSPHERE OF THE BAR IN A VILLAGE PUB – THIS IS IT. Harry Cox (left) and Walter Hubbard enjoyed a pint in a corner of the bar in "The Plough" several decades ago. (HB)

23 YEAR OLD 2ND LIEUTENANT JEAN ANDERSON OF U.S. AIR FORCE WHO LOST HIS LIFE ON 26TH APRIL 1945 IN STAYING AT THE CONTROLS OF HIS BOMBER WHEN IT SEEMED LIKELY THAT IT WOULD CRASH ON WHITNASH.

Part of the 406th Bombardment Squadron, based at the AAF station at Harrington, Northamptonshire, Pilot Anderson and 9 other crew members set out on their 7th mission which was to drop propaganda leaflets in north-western Germany, a few weeks before the end of the Second World War in Europe.

Shortly after 9 p.m. the bomber became uncontrollable because of icing and when the ailerons locked at 6,000 feet the crew were ordered to bale out. Pilot Anderson himself was ready to jump, but in waiting to save the lives of Whitnash inhabitants, on whose houses the plane seemed likely to crash, he left it too late. The bomber crashed into a field near Ashford Road, a huge crater being gouged out by the wreckage, which was still smoking next morning. Rushing outside after the crash, villagers were amazed to see the 9 survivors floating down on parachutes, one later being entangled in a tree in the Tachbrook Road.

Jean Anderson's remains were buried in the American Cemetery in Cambridge and posthumously he was awarded the Purple Heart for Military Merit. (GC)

"MISSION ACCOMPLISHED" – 39 YEARS LATER. GERALD COX AND GAIL ANDERSON ADMIRE THE NAME BOARD OF ANDERSON DRIVE.

As a 16 year old youth, Gerald Cox witnessed the crash and it made a very deep impression on him and others. Within months, Gerald had written to the brave pilot's parents in Mason, Michigan and they had written a very moving reply including the words, "We are proud to be the parents of the pilot whom your people consider an International hero. This does not lessen our grief, but makes it easier to bear."

A year later, at Christmas 1946, Mr and Mrs Anderson were writing to Gerald about "Our boy who now sleeps in England."

Gerald Cox and Keith Douglas of Dorridge, Solihull, both tried to have the pilot honoured. Eventually on the 39th Anniversary of the fatal crash, Gerald's efforts were rewarded and a new road, situated only 100 yards from the site of the crash, was named Anderson Drive. The unveiling of the name board was carried out by Lt. Col. Fred Bush, Assistant Air Attaché in London, on 26th April 1984, the dead pilot's younger brother Gail and his wife Donna flying from Michigan for the ceremony. (Photograph — Leamington Spa Courier)

ANOTHER KEEN FOOTBALL TEAM WAS THE WHITNASH DYNAMOS OF 1945.

From left to right the players were – BACK Alan Markham, Derrick Seekings, Eric Davis, John Hancock, and David Murray. MIDDLE Jim Wright, John Munnery, Stan Parker, Bill Bench, Bob Edwards, and Gerald Cox. FRONT Keith Walton and Graham Adams.

Several members of this team have lived in Whitnash all their lives and in 1983 a reunion was organised. The intervening 38 years rolled away as the entire team posed for other photographs. (GC)

THIS HANDSOME ALSATION WAS RINTY, WHO BELONGED TO THE FELGATE FAMILY IN THE SHOP IN HEATHCOTE ROAD. This faithful dog would accompany the children in his family to the village school, going to meet them every afternoon. He kept up this daily routine for years, even though as he grew older and more arthritic, he could barely keep up on the way home. He was one of the most faithful and best behaved dogs I have ever known and in this photograph he is sitting in the playing field near Acre Close; the tall chimney in the background being that at A.P.

However perhaps the most famous dog in Whitnash was Mr Palmer's old English sheepdog Bob. In the 1950s, when his master had finished with his services for the day, Bob would go his rounds – making numerous calls at houses round the village, hoping for tasty titbits. Strangers would gape amazed as he pushed open the garden gates of sympathetic householders and barked outside the front door. If nothing was available in those days of meat shortages, a shake of the head and a "Nothing today Bob" would suffice and he would trot off to his next call. Whenever Mr Palmer went to Leamington with his horse and trap or when he cycled, Bob would lollop along beside him and in the summer Bob became unrecognisable when he had his annual haircut; all his thick coat being cut off, except for huge ruff s round his paws. (IB)

THE HEATHCOTE INN WAS ERECTED JUST PRIOR TO THE SECOND WORLD WAR AND BEARS THE DATE 1940 ON A WALL. During the war the building was requisitioned as accommodation for army personnel and it is said that a Home Guard Platoon used to drill in the room now the bar. Mrs C. Hayman, who has lived nearby for many years, described to me how the building had been enlarged over the years. Both she and Mr Hadfield of Heathcote Road recalled that when the inn opened after the war, one of the first licensees was appropriately named Mr Churchill. (JF)

VILLAGE FETES WERE A GREAT SOURCE OF ENTERTAINMENT IN PAST DECADES AND TO BE CHOSEN AS "MISS WHITNASH" AND TO PRESIDE OVER THE FESTIVITIES WAS CONSIDERED A GREAT HONOUR. This snap shows Miss Vilma Avis, proudly displaying the "Miss Whitnash" sash in 1947.

Garden fetes were often held in the Rectory Garden and on September 3rd 1938 the Parish Magazine promised "Bowling for a Leg of Mutton (ladies) and for a Ham (gentlemen)" amongst the other attractions. Admission was 4d (tickets purchased before the day 3d) and Teas were provided at 9d each.

A party held to celebrate the end of the First World War in 1918, was remembered by Fred Meades. A long barn near Home Farm was festooned with streamers and in the sports, which took place in the field now the site of Home Farm Crescent, he won a tankard for running. (GC)

THE HOMESTEAD FARMHOUSE IN 1958. THE SAGGING THATCH GAVE THIS SEVENTEENTH CENTURY BUILDING AN AIR OF MYSTERY. Old "Tad" Palmer, the last remaining member of a once powerful family, lived here alone, tending the few animals which provided him with an income. This typical old-time farmer, with mud-spattered, leather gaiters, sometimes seemed lonely, but his animals always seemed pleased to see him.

When Robert Brain Palmer eventually died in June 1965 at the age of 78, fittingly he was the last to be buried in the actual churchyard in Whitnash, a plot having been reserved alongside other family members. (IB)

CAREFUL COMPARISON OF THE BEAMS WILL CONFIRM THAT THIS ELEGANT HOUSE NOW KNOWN AS "ELDERFIELD" IS INDEED THE HOMESTEAD FARMHOUSE, AFTER BEING RE-ROOFED AND RENOVATED IN 1959.

Each time I cycle past I am always amused to note that part of the old wall still skirts the garden. As I pass the wooden door set into this wall, I half expect to see Tad emerge, with Bob as usual at his heels, to walk across to his stable which was next to Glamis Cottage. (JF)

THIS CONTENTED SOW IS GRAZING IN THE ORCHARD BELONGING TO MR PALMER AT HOMESTEAD FARM (NOW ELDERFIELD). Taken in the 1940s, this snap shows Home Farm in the background.

One of the earliest domesticated animals, the pig is said to be very intelligent. In the days before intensive farming, bacon took weeks, sometimes months, to cure, but it was full of flavour when eaten. Sometimes huge sides of maturing bacon, hanging from hooks in the ceiling, could be glimpsed through the windows of Mr Palmer's kitchen. I once saw them myself and was most impressed.

This snap will remind many people of a different concept of farming, before many animals were condemned to exist in tiny pens and the bacon-curing processes were speeded up because accountants insisted on quick profits. (FG)

THE SNOWFALL EXPERIENCED IN 1947 HAS BECOME LEGENDARY AND THIS UNUSUAL VIEW, TAKEN IN THAT YEAR, SHOWS HOME FARM, WITH THE OLD BARN AND STABLING IN FRONT. The photograph was taken down the lane opposite (now Home Farm Crescent) where the huge banks of snow can be seen on either side.

Before it was demolished in 1958, the barn caused the road to curve – in effect making a blind corner. This was always known as "Freddy's Corner", presumably because at some time, Freddy had met with an accident there. Who Freddy was, I have never been able to discover, but I used to imagine that he was a poor child, knocked down by a fast horse and trap, which had been unable to stop in time.

(HB)

CONTENTED COWS QUIETLY GRAZING; A MEADOW STUDDED WITH BUTTERCUPS AND A PASSING STEAM TRAIN – WHAT MORE DELIGHTFUL SCENE COULD THERE BE? No doubt some Whitnash residents of today will be amazed to learn that this (slightly slanting) photograph was taken in the early 1950s, from the end of the lane opposite to Home Farm; more or less where the row of shops in Home Farm Crescent is today. Between 1956 and 1960, the buttercups disappeared and houses in Home Farm Crescent and Canon Young Road were built on the field. (IB)

THIS VIEW OF "APPLETREE COTTAGE" IN THE DOGLANDS WAS PHOTOGRAPHED IN THE 1950s. Today the cottage remains much as it was, but the field shown here is now occupied by houses in Palmer Road and bungalows and garages in The Doglands. The somewhat rough pasture and huge bramble patch reminds me of so many other similar fields, long since built upon, in which I played as a child. (IB)

THIS FINE ELM TREE HAS NOW GONE, BUT THE WALL REMAINS. Taken in 1959 from a corner of Home farm Crescent, this winter snapshot shows the half-timbered house in the process of being renovated.

This elm was typical of the many that once grew in Whitnash. In 1865 Canon Young wrote, "The timber from these Whitnash elms used in former years to command a higher price than from any other place in the neighbourhood." Certainly elm wood was very useful being partially water resistant and because of this it was the wood generally used for making coffins.

The late Mr P. Simmonds (Son) a native of Tachbrook, told me last year how he used to help the Sexton, seventy years ago. It was customary when digging a double grave, to place a thick board of elm over the coffin. Then when the grave was opened, digging was far easier and the first coffin was not disturbed. In Whitnash, as in most villages, it was customary for the village carpenter to make the coffins and arrange funerals. Mrs Gibbs of Avon Road told me how her late husband used to help the carpenter, Mr Summerton, over 50 years ago, to move the coffins which had been made in a workshop in the garden. (IB)

THIS GROUP OF BELL-RINGERS AT ST MARGARET'S CHURCH IN 1956 SHOWS THE FAMOUS MR FREDERICK HAULEY, THEN AGED 90, IN THE CENTRE OF THE FRONT ROW. From 1919, until shortly before his death in 1963 at the age of 97. Mr Hauley was a regular chorister and bell-ringer at St Margaret's and he did much to encourage the younger ringers by making charts to render complicated changes easier. Towards the end of his life he was featured in many newspaper articles as one of the oldest bell ringers in the world and this ex-post office worker was indeed an interesting man.

The others in this photograph are from left to right – BACK Ian Maycock, Fred Farmer (a carpenter who made various items for the church), unknown, Michael Cockburn. MIDDLE unknown, Glen Hales, Margaret Dee, Percy Oram (Captain of the tower), Ruth Morby, Rev. Gleave (Rector) Judith Williams, John Height. FRONT Christine Saunders, Jean Addicott, Ann Trindall, Yvonne Oram (Percy Oram's daughter). (JP)

THE LOCAL "COURIER" OF SEPTEMBER 7TH 1956 CARRIED A REPORT ON THE OPENING OF THE NEW COUNTY JUNIOR SCHOOL IN LANGLEY ROAD, TOGETHER WITH THIS PHOTOGRAPH OF THE BUILDINGS.

Previously 239 children aged 5 to 11 had been accommodated in 5 different buildings in Whitnash, as the old school premises proved totally inadequate. St Margaret's Hall, the W.I. Hut and The New Hall had all being used as temporary accommodation and organisation was a nightmare.

These new buildings cost £50,000 and 200 children and 8 teachers arrived on the first morning. Mr Whitmarsh was the Headmaster, Mr Skerritt the Deputy Head and the assistant teachers were Mrs Barnes, Miss West, Mrs Clarke, Miss Jeffes, Mrs Markham, Mr Hoyle and Mrs Lambert. Six teachers were authorised "to inflict corporal punishment according to the Committee's regulations."

The school log-book contained some amusing details. On the first day no paper towels had been delivered and four ordinary towels were made available for the pupils. On the 4th day the paper towels arrived, but the secretary had to wait around a month for her typewriter.

Over the years, there have been several extensions built and today Whitnash Combined School occupies the buildings. With Ms June Malcolm as the head teacher, there are 300 pupils on roll. (WCRO)

ONE OF MY FAVOURITE PHOTOGRAPHS FROM THE WHOLE COLLECTION; 5019 "TREAGO CASTLE" WITH THE 10.00 BIRMINGHAM SNOW HILL TO PADDINGTON TRAIN PASSING UNDER BLACK BRIDGE. The photograph was taken by R. J. Blenkinsop on 9th September 1958 and one can almost feel the movement as the smoke and steam clear and Black Bridge once again becomes visible.

During the late nineteen forties and fifties, many of us spent most of our spare time train-spotting and chatting on or near Black Bridge. The wonderful combination of colours, noises, smells and vibrations thrilled me enormously as locomotives such as 6998 "Burton Agnes Hall," 5008 "Raglan Castle" or 5082 "Swordfish" disturbed the peace of the country lane.

The total Whitnash area is perhaps best observed from a train, as the railway follows the more remote areas near the brook till the Fosse Way boundary is passed. I often travel to London by train and each time I marvel at the unspoilt countryside in south Whitnash. (Photograph by R. J. Blenkinsop)

THIS WINTER SNAP OF THE ANCIENT ELM ON THE VILLAGE GREEN WAS TAKEN IN 1959, NOT LONG BEFORE THE TREE WAS REMOVED ON THE ORDERS OF THE PARISH COUNCIL WHO WISHED TO MODERNISE THE AREA. The Council had assumed responsibility for the care of the village green (previously held by the Lord of the Manor) and members said they had had complaints that children committed nuisances inside the hollow.

Soon a tremendous row ensued between residents who wished to keep the tree and those who did not. H. W. Box (dubbed the Lieutenant of the 'Save the Tree Corps') drew up a petition and a public meeting called by the Council to discuss the matter voted 49 to 1 to retain the tree. People such as Sydney Addicott of Heathcote Road and Ivy Bailey of Tachbrook Road wrote letters to the local newspapers insisting that the tree be kept and local television stations and even national newspapers carried reports on the row. The Bishop of Coventry, and local County Councillor William Wilson, a solicitor, (now the longest serving member of the County Council) both expressed opinions, but the Council refused to budge and on the afternoon of Friday 8th January 1960, an excavator demolished the tree. I wrote in my diary that evening, "I feel as if an old friend has gone" and ever afterwards my father counted the loss of the elm as one of his greatest disappointments. Had the protective railings not been removed during the Second World War, it might have been a different story. (IB)

THIRTY OR FORTY YEARS AGO 'DARBY AND JOAN' GROUPS USED TO HAVE REGULAR MEETINGS IN THE WOMEN'S INSTITUTE HUT, SITUATED NEAR "THE PLOUGH AND HARROW." This photograph, taken in the 1950s, has some real characters in the line-up. From left to right, the near table is Jack Warr, Mrs Lawrence, Mrs Place (better known as Granny Place – the school dinner lady) and Mrs Hemmings in the satin blouse.

I remember Mrs Hemmings in particular for on Coronation Day in 1953, as it was wet, she and others entertained our group in "The New Hall" with songs and recitations. Her rendering of the Longfellow poem "Under a spreading chestnut tree, the village smithy stands, / The smith a mighty man is he, with large and sinewy hands," was unforgettable; her robust actions making us cry with laughter. After Mr Lancaster had performed "Burlington Bertie" and told jokes we munched our way through piles of jam tarts and thoroughly enjoyed ourselves.

The W.I. Hut had been officially opened in November 1936 by Lady Bird and it was often hired for parties and meetings. My twenty-first birthday party was held there, so I have happy memories of it. (GC)

ROSABEL THE GOAT ON THE RECTORY LAWN AROUND 1950.

Whilst Rev. Gleave was Rector, goats were kept which grazed on the extensive grass areas at the Rectory. Rosabel, Wasabel, Daisybel, Clarabel, Snowbel, and Marybel formed the Bel Herd and they were mainly white British Saanan goats, except one which was an Anglo-Nubian (a brown and white goat with floppy ears) and one which was a Toggenberg. Any excess milk was turned into yoghurt (then only available from Health Food shops) or cream cheese.

For this information I am indebted to Margaret, the daughter of Rev. Gleave (now Mrs Lomas).

The two fine elm trees in the background were typical of those in the Whitnash area – in fact some books refer to the elm as "The Warwickshire Weed" and claim that the word Leam is derived from "Leamhain" an ancient word meaning "Water of the Elms." (IB)

DERRICK SEEKINGS AND FLO PLACE IN "THIS HAPPY BREED" – ONE OF THE MANY EXCELLENT PLAYS PRODUCED BY 'THE WHITNASH PLAYERS' This particular play in 1953 was chosen as being appropriate for Coronation Year, but since 1946 dozens of dramas and comedies have entertained the residents of Whitnash.

Their first play was "Without the Prince", at St Margaret's Hall in 1946, but a keen company of people such as Albert Townsend, Peggy, Bert and Joan Seekings, Ken and Ida Wakefield, Freddy Place, Jean Hall, Les and Dorothy Burrows, Tom Shakespeare, Tom Commander and many more too numerous to mention, produced up to three plays a year. From 1949 productions were in "The New Hall" and from 1974 in The Community Centre. Enthusiastic members such as Norman Coles, Caroline and Chris Sheard, Valerie O'Keefe, Marion and Wilf Poultney, Hazel Byrne and Mary Squires carried on the fine tradition of the company and the latest play was "Confusions" by Alan Ayckbourn in 1992.

Derrick Seekings joked recently, "I must have been in over one hundred plays, but I have always enjoyed taking part." (GC)

IN 1955 THE THEN PRIME MINISTER ADDRESSED A PUBLIC MEETING IN THIS HALL. This recent photograph hardly does justice to "The New Hall", once the centre of social life in Whitnash, but since the building of the Community Centre in 1974, relegated to being an additional room for the adjoining Social Club.

In 1948 a much needed field for sports had been purchased and in 1949 "The New Hall" (a second-hand, prefabricated building) was erected, thanks initially to people such as Bob Hall. In the early days the sports field lacked any amenities and I recall helping keen cricketer John Yarwood create a practice wicket with a hand mower and borrowed garden roller.

The hall was used for a variety of events and prior to the General Elections of 1951 and 1955, Sir Anthony Eden (M.P. for Warwick and Leamington from 1923) and others addressed public meetings there. Much amusement was caused on one occasion because a joking gardener outside shouted the popular radio catchphrase of the day "When are you going to do something for the workers?" An immaculate lady helper who had overheard, tried in all innocence to make Sir Anthony answer this question! In 1955, on the resignation of Sir Winston Churchill, Sir Anthony Eden became Prime Minister and for two years, local constituents were very privileged. (JF)

PRESIDENT MICHAEL MORRIS OUTSIDE THE SPORTS AND SOCIAL CLUB.

In 1958 it was decided to raise funds by selling £1 shares for a Social Club and volunteers, on a shoe-string budget, gradually built a hall, bar and other rooms. Albert Bean of Franklin Road (now 91 but still able to enjoy a drink there) told me how he had been in charge of the original building. As to the volunteer workers – "Some were good, some not so good, but all were willing," he remarked wryly. The steel was salvaged from Ashorne Hill and wood for the seating from the demolished Christchurch in Leamington, but skill and ingenuity made them serviceable. Local builders Mr Montgomery and Mr Duggins were supportive and the Social Club opened in July 1959; the first Chairman being Dave Perrot and Secretary John Honey.

Later other amenities such as tennis courts and bowling greens were added and today there are 860 members. Appropriately the President is Michael Morris, the genial and astute long-serving Town Councillor and past member of the Warwick Rural District Council and County Council.

Raising money for charity has long been a tradition (years ago George Billington used to sing "The Royal Warwickshires" whilst people threw coppers on the floor) but in recent years five Guide Dog Puppies have been paid for largely by a Domino League.

(JF)

THIS DELIGHTFUL CORNER OF WHITNASH STILL EXISTS, ALTHOUGH THE LANE HAS BEEN WIDENED AND MUCH OF THE GREENERY HAS DISAPPEARED. Taken in the 1950s, facing Whitnash Road, this photograph shows Cooks Cottages on the right and the large house in the Doglands on the left. The barn in the background belonged to Bill Masters at Green Farm and today the site in Whitnash Road is occupied by three houses. (HB)

MR H. W. BOX PROUDLY HOLDS THE WHITNASH CHAIRMAN'S BADGE FOR WHICH HE DID THE RESEARCH AND ORIGINAL DESIGN. THE BADGE, COSTING £70, WAS PAID FOR BY FOUR ANONYMOUS DONORS AND ON 13TH MARCH 1964, IT WAS FORMALLY PRESENTED TO THE CHAIRMAN OF WHITNASH PARISH COUNCIL, MR C. MULLARD, BY COUNCILLOR MRS ELIZABETH HUME, CHAIRMAN OF WARWICK DISTRICT COUNCIL.

A headline in the Leamington Spa Courier at that time read "Badge of Independence" and so it is today for Bernard Kirton, the first Mayor, uses the same badge on a modified chain.

The symbols on the badge represent features of Whitnash history. The five-barred gate denotes the fact that Whitnash was one of the last places to have the open fields enclosed in 1851 and the open book at the bottom represents one of the first parish magazines in the country. The bell and wavy lines illustrate the legend of the loss of the bell in the well near the brook and the sheaves of corn indicate the fertile nature of the soil. The trees and border of leaves of course represent the famous elm trees.

During the recent twinning festivities, the municipal magazine of the French town Villebon carried a full page about Whitnash, including details of the badge. "Le blason de Whitnash" sounded most interesting and I am sure my father would have been very proud. (Photograph — Leamington Spa Courier)

PICTURESQUE ST MARGARET'S HAS ALWAYS BEEN POPULAR FOR WEDDINGS AND I HOPE THIS PHOTOGRAPH BRINGS BACK HAPPY MEMORIES FOR HUNDREDS OF COUPLES WHO WERE MARRIED THERE.

The emotive moment when the bride arrives at the church, attended by apprehensive, colourfully-clad bridesmaids is beautifully captured in this unusual photograph taken on 23rd June 1962. The radiant June bride was Valerie Taylor, seen on the arm of her father Blain and bridesmaid Carole Jacobs (left) was next to Matron of Honour Margaret Lomas (née Gleave) with bridesmaid Andrea Taylor to the right. Valerie married Michael Jacobs of Heathcote Road and as she had been a bell ringer for a number of years, she entered the church through the belfry door, decorated with bells, ribbons and greenery, as was the custom at weddings of the ringers. The Rector happily waiting to greet the party was Rev. Gleave. (VJ)

EVERYONE SEEMS TO BE ENJOYING THEMSELVES AT ST MARGARET'S CHOIR DINNER IN 1966. From the left the back row is – Unknown, Neville Rainford, Brian Burrows, Ian Box, Peter Jackson, Simon Yarwood, David Moffat, Gilbert Turner and Paul Yarwood. The front row is Mr Mold (Lay Reader) Rev. Mallet, Rev. Gleave (Rector) George Pratt (Organist) and Bill Higgins.

The choir at St Margaret's has a long tradition, although they did not wear surplices until the 1880s. In 1872, the Whitnash Choral Society gave a concert in the Garden House at the Rectory, but the Parish Magazine later reported, "Some of the performers were rather late in their attendance, owing to detention in the hay field". I was much amused by this statement, but in a rural community, farm work took precedence over almost everything.

During the 1920s, Fred Meades and George Billington recalled being paid 1/6d per month as choirboys and if any boy committed a misdemeanour, he was suspended. One boy, on receiving such punishment, threw a half-brick at the church clock, damaging the minute hand.

In fairly recent times there have been tales of the false teeth of an over-zealous, middle-aged chorister flying across the chancel in mid-hymn and of choristers who missed their cue for a solo and joined in several bars behind the organ – the discord giving some members of the congregation hysterics. Thomas Hardy's errant choir at Longpuddle had nothing on the Whitnash choir!

Today an enthusiastic group of both sexes carry on the fine tradition for good church music. (IB)

IN 1869 THE FREE METHODISTS OPENED THIS ONE-ROOMED BUILDING, ADJOINING FIELD VIEWS. Bought by the Wesleyans in 1893, for many years the building was much used, but by 1950 so many repairs were needed that the congregation decided to hold services in "The New Hall". This photograph was taken in 1952, shortly before the old chapel was demolished. Eventually two flats were built on the site. (GC)

THE NEW METHODIST CHURCH IN MURCOTT ROAD WAS DEDICATED ON 14TH OCTOBER 1967. The minister was Rev. A. Baxter and many gifts enabled the attractive church to be well equipped; Mr and Mrs Bodfish giving an organ in memory of their teenage son Philip who had been killed in a road accident. In 1992 25th Anniversary celebrations were held; happily Rev. A. Baxter being able to join the present minister Rev. Michael Sawyer in leading the lively congregation. (JF)

ST JOSEPH'S ROMAN CATHOLIC CHURCH IN MURCOTT ROAD WAS BUILT IN 1971, THE FIRST MASS BEING CELEBRATED ON THE FEAST OF CHRIST THE KING BY FATHER JOSEPH MCKENNA, THE PARISH PRIEST. THE BUILDING WAS BLESSED AND DEDICATED ON 12TH DECEMBER 1971 BY THE MOST REVEREND G. P. DWYER, ARCHBISHOP OF BIRMINGHAM. The church is an imaginative, modern building and the entrance hall contains a most unusual wall sculpture in brick by Walter Richie depicting "The Flight Into Eygpt". I found a stained glass window commemorating in 1975 the Canonisation of Saint Oliver Plunkett, who had been martyred at Tyburn in 1681, very interesting as was a plaque to Katherine Agnes Underhill. A benefactress of that church, she died in January 1990 aged 79.

St Joseph's Infant and Junior School in Rowley Road was opened in April 1966 and the 96 pupils had 3 teachers, Mr Layton being the head master. In 1991 the school celebrated its 25th Anniversary and on 27th November a 25th Anniversary Mass, celebrated by Bishop Brain, was attended by present and past pupils.

Today the head teacher is Michael Duggan who was appointed in 1985 and at present there are 205 pupils on roll. (JF)

THE POPULAR LONG-SERVING ORGANIST AT ST MARGARET'S, MR G. L. PRATT IS PICTURED SHORTLY BEFORE HIS RETIREMENT IN 1984. As a boy George Pratt sang in the choir at Holy Trinity Church in Leamington Spa, where he was taught to play the organ by the famous S. F. Bates. Now aged 84, George described to me recently how Whitnash Church had only gas lighting when he became organist and choirmaster in 1934. A much respected musician who enhanced St Margaret's reputation for fine music, he held the post for 50 years.

The organ in St Margaret's installed new in 1857 is a fine quality instrument made by J. W. Walker & Co. Costing £140, it was donated by Edward Wood of Newbold Revel and it was first played on October 29th 1857, the birthday of the only son of the donor. Originally positioned in the Vestry adjoining the chancel, the organ was moved to the rear of the church in 1967. (WCRO)

IN 1989 EXTENSIONS TO ST MARGARET'S CHURCH WERE COMPLETED AND THE RECTOR, CANON A. GARDNER, LOOKED JUSTIFIABLY PROUD OF THE NORTH TRANSEPT. A modern, octagonal Chapter House was also built, but thanks to the skill of the architect John Holmes both new additions blended in well with the older parts of the church.

In 1993, Canon Gardner celebrates his 25th Anniversary as Rector of Whitnash. This tall, locally-born man, whose interests include golf, ocean cruises and steam trains, has presided over many changes in the church and his integrity, sincerity and good humour have won him many friends. (I am grateful to Mr W. Bailey for the loan of this photograph.)

(Photograph — Coventry Evening Telegraph)

ALTHOUGH THIS PHOTOGRAPH WAS TAKEN AROUND THIRTY YEARS AGO, ONLY WITHIN THE LAST FIVE YEARS HAS THIS AREA CHANGED DRAMATICALLY. The brick walls and orchard, which once belonged to Watts Cottages (shown right) have only recently been replaced by St Margaret's House (Retirement Homes) close to the church. (IB)

IN RECENT TIMES THERE HAVE BEEN SEVERAL INSTANCES OF HOW BRAVE WHITNASH RESIDENTS HAVE OVERCOME PHYSICAL HANDICAPS. ONE SUCH STORY IS THAT OF JENNIFER SCANLON.

When she was born in September 1975, Jenny had a serious heart complaint and as a small child she was often extremely ill. However she was determined to attend school like the others and at the beginning of her first term on September 10th 1980, she was delighted to discover that she was the 1,000th pupil to be admitted to Briar Hill County First School. The newly appointed head teacher, Mrs Sarah Lancaster, had arranged a reception and brave Jenny was given flowers and a certificate. This photograph was taken on that occasion, with the rest of the pupils and staff watching Mrs Lancaster and her five year old pupil.

The happy ending to this story is that in February 1988, Jenny was lucky enough to have a heart and lung transplant at Harefield Hospital and is now fit and well. She is studying at Campion School, but still lives close to Briar Hill, so she is able to keep in contact.

First opened in 1970, Briar Hill First School now has 284 pupils on the roll and Mrs Lancaster is in her thirteenth year as head teacher.

(Photograph — Leamington Spa Courier)

WITHIN THE PAST YEAR THERE HAS BEEN AN EVENT OF GREAT HISTORICAL INTEREST FOR IN SEPTEMBER 1992, THE TOWN COUNCIL VOTED TO APPOINT COUNCILLOR BERNARD KIRTON (THEN CHAIRMAN) AS THE FIRST MAYOR OF WHITNASH.

Having lived in the same house in Avon Road in Whitnash for over 30 years and having been very active in local politics for almost all of that time, Yorkshire-born, ex-Merchant Naval Officer, Mr Kirton was a popular choice for the honour. He had represented the residents of Whitnash on the Parish Council, District Council and County Council for many years and in 1977 had been the youngest ever Chairman of Warwick District Council. Although everyone involved in local politics has their critics, Councillor Kirton being no exception, all agree that he has worked very hard for Whitnash for many years, giving freely of his time, energy and considerable debating talents for the benefit of his constituents.

Like Councillor Morris, the Deputy Mayor, Mr Kirton long ago had a road named after him. Close examination of the road names of Whitnash show that for around 25 years, long-serving members of the council have been similarly honoured, as have long-serving residents in other spheres, for instance Whitnash-born Jean Clarkson (née Billington) who has been "Brown Owl" with the 1st Whitnash Brownies for over 30 years. Unlike some towns, almost all the road names in Whitnash have local connections and this would seem to re-inforce the idea that, like Canon Young, the Whitnash people of today are proud of their past and their present. (Photograph — John Wright Photography)

IN 1992 THE MORNING SERVICE AT ST MARGARET'S ON REMEMBRANCE SUNDAY CONCLUDED WITH AN ACT OF REMEMBRANCE ROUND THE WAR MEMORIAL, AS CAN BE SEEN IN THIS PHOTOGRAPH. Following a number of years when the service had been conducted inside, in the year when Whitnash first had a Mayor, it was felt appropriate for part of the service once again to be held on the ancient village green.

It was a moving service with Deputy Mayor, Michael Morris, reading out the names of those who had died – H. Allibone, A. T. Batchelor, E. E. Batchelor, S. R. Biffin, H. Butler, G. D. W. Chimes, A. Duckett, A. G. Mann, J. Owen and F. E. Parker in the First World War and E. Boneham, W. H. Hughes, C. H. Hubbard, F. W. Lancaster, A. Osborne, A. T. Sutton and D. J. Wright in the Second World War. The Mayor, Bernard Kirton, laid a wreath and said the familiar and moving words "They shall grow not old as we that are left grow old," after the customary period of silence.

As I stood there in the chilly morning air, I thought particularly of F. W. Lancaster for during the 1950s I had become friendly with his father, a retired railway guard who had a passion for horse racing. Despite his jovial manner, Mr Lancaster never seemed to forget the loss of his son and neither I suppose did the other bereaved families. (JF)

IN OCTOBER 1992, WHITNASH ENTERTAINED THE MAYORS FROM VILLEBONSUR-YVETTE IN FRANCE AND WEILERSWIST IN GERMANY. The occasion was the signing of an official twinning document between Whitnash and the other towns. The three mayors each placed a wreath on the war memorial and later presented prizes to the schoolchildren who had designed the winning posters in a competition to advertise the occasion.

THIS PHOTOGRAPH SHOWS FROM LEFT TO RIGHT – (BACK ROW) BERNARD KIRTON, Mayor of Whitnash; GUENTER ROSENKE, Mayor of Weilerswist; GERARD NEVERS, Mayor of Villebon. (MIDDLE ROW) KATIE SMITH aged 10 from St Margaret's School; VIKI FRANKLIN aged 11 from Whitnash Combined School. (FRONT ROW) KATIE POTTER aged 10 from St Joseph's School; DAWN GARDENER aged 8 from Briar Hill School. (Photograph — Leamington Spa Observer)

Personal Thoughts

Everyone has their own particular memories of a place and this book has traced mine. If I have omitted to mention some of the memories which various people were kind enough to share with me, I apologise, but in a book of this size, I had, of necessity, to be selective. I am only too aware of the people I have not mentioned at all – people such as Percy Greville Smith (the trilby-clad Councillor who used to walk round the village on a Sunday morning in case anyone had any complaints), Mr Brain (a champion hedgecutter), J. Schofield (capped several times for Wales and who began the Whitnash Rugby Club), May Stretton (a woodcarver), Mr and Mrs Robbins (she was a Sunday School teacher for 54 years), Harry Hughes (the village bobby for many years), Denis Jacobs, Mrs Maycock, Sidney Tew and many more. I have done my best to create a picture, albeit a sketchy one, but I have almost enough material for two books.

Sadly the mature elms are all dead – killed by dutch elm disease or the developer's chainsaw, but some things in Whitnash are the same as they ever were. There are many caring people still doing their best to carry on the fine traditions of the past and many more children now have a great interest in the town where they live.

This is the first book of any size to be produced exclusively about Whitnash for nearly 130 years, since Canon Young wrote his history in 1865. Obviously his book was extremely useful, but the more modern history I have had to piece together myself.

Few people remember today that in 1964 there was a proposal for the creation of a "super borough" of Leamington, by amalgamation with Warwick and the absorption of various districts such as Whitnash. Following meetings for discussion, the twelve members of the Parish Council – C. Mullard (Chairman), H. W. Box (Vice-Chairman), B. J. Lane, M. J. Morris, B. V. Marchant, J. R. A. Armstrong, P. G. Smith, D. Hooley, H. L. Burrows, F. V. Place, F. E. Yeomans and K. F. Tunnicliff, with J. Bullock as Parish Clerk, put out a forthright and well planned statement saying that Whitnash wanted none of the proposals. Many believe that it was the clear and vociferous objections put forward by Whitnash that helped to kill the proposals in due course. As the only member of that council still serving, Mr Morris is to be congratulated.

The statement put out by the council in 1964 received much publicity. "To let this beautiful village, with its old and new buildings be absorbed into Leamington Borough would be utter sacrilege. It would lose its ancient link with the past and its individual identity would be lost forever, if government was from Leamington by councillors not in touch with the needs of the parish."

Echoes of this statement have come from Councillor Kirton, the first Mayor. Recently he said that he thought that the greatest asset which Whitnash possessed was its sense of community identity. The roots of this modern spirit of independence would seem to lie far in the past, for the more I researched the history the more convinced I became that for numerous centuries, people had been immensely proud of living in Whitnash.

Appendix

THE RECTORS OF WHITNASH

1300 Simon de Rideswell
1302 Henry de Compton
1326 Osbert de Banbury
1332 Thomas de Brayles
1336 William de Wigorn
In 1349 John de Whitnash was Vicar of Radford
1352 William Comyn, de Newbold
1358 William de Souche
1372 William de Feryby
1378 John Brigstock
1393 Thomas Durich
1398 John de Magna Cotes
1406 John Normanby
1445 William Smyth
1453 Richard de Gaydon
1483 Robert Beverley
1492 Richard Bennet (also Vicar of Leamington)
1534 Edward Bolyfant
1554 Humphrey Weyring
1572 Ralph Kent
1609 Nicholas Greenhill
1650 Thomas Holyoke
1675 Richard Byles
1690 Emmanuel Langford
Richard Farmer
1732 Thomas Morse
1786 Charles Woolsey Johnson
1829 Edward Willes
1833 Charles Samuel Twisleton
1842 Leopold Erasmus Dryden
1846 James Reynolds Young
1884 Alexander Hugh Monckton Russell
1919 Claude Alexander Hugh Russell
1923 Edward William Bryan
1935 Charles Haughton Gleave
1968 Anthony Brian Gardner

POPULATION

1086	-112	1911	-525
1290	-150	1921	-570
1665	-112	1931	-586
1730	-168	1951	-1,682
1811	-203	1961	-4,486
1821	-260	1971	-6,198
1831	-273	1977	-6,912
1841	-313	1981	-7,235
1851	-346	1986	-7,267
1861	-392	1991	-7,297 (2,768 houses)
1881	-426		
1891	-520		

AREA

1865 – 1,242 acres.
1951 – 1,239 acres.
1991 – 1,193 acres. (483 Hectares)

BY THE SAME AUTHOR

A Tour of St Margaret's Church Whitnash
Published 1992 (obtainable from the church).

She Dyed About Midnight (Warwick)
Published 1992 by Brewin Books.